MOONTIDE

Niall Campbell was born in 1984 on the island of South Uist, one of the Outer Hebrides of Scotland. He received an Eric Gregory Award in 2011 and an Arvon-Jerwood Mentorship in 2013, and won the *Poetry London* Competition in 2013. His work has been published in a number of magazines and anthologies including, *Granta, The Dark Horse, Poetry London, Poetry Review, The Salt Book of Younger Poets* and *Best Scottish Poems 2011.* His debut pamphlet, *After the Creel Fleet,* was published by Happenstance Press in 2012. His first book-length collection, *Moontide* (Bloodaxe Books, 2014), won Britain's biggest poetry prize, the £20,000 Edwin Morgan Poetry Award, as well as the Saltire Scottish First Book of the Year Award, and is a Poetry Book Society Recommendation. It was also shortlisted for the Forward Prize for Best First Collection and the Fenton Aldeburgh First Collection Prize. He lives in Edinburgh.

NIALL CAMPBELL

MOONTIDE

BLOODAXE BOOKS

Copyright © Niall Campbell 2014

ISBN: 978 1 78037 118 4

First published 2014 by
Bloodaxe Books Ltd,
Eastburn,
South Park,
Hexham,
Northumberland NE46 1BS.

Reprinted 2014 (twice)

www.bloodaxebooks.com
For further information about Bloodaxe titles
please visit our website or write to
the above address for a catalogue.

Supported by
**ARTS COUNCIL
ENGLAND**

Cover design: Neil Astley & Pamela Robertson-Pearce.

Printed in Great Britain by Bell & Bain Limited, Glasgow, Scotland, on
acid-free paper sourced from mills with FSC chain of custody certification.

ACKNOWLEDGEMENTS

Acknowledgments are due to the editors of the following journals and anthologies in which some of these poems have previously appeared: *Best British Poetry 2013*, *Best Scottish Poems 2011*, *BODY*, *The Bow-Wow Shop*, *The Dark Horse*, *Granta*, *The Herald*, *Magma*, *New Linear Perspectives*, *Northwords Now*, *Oxford Poetry*, *POEM*, *Poetry London*, *Poetry Review*, *The Rialto*, *The Red Wheelbarrow*, *The Salt Book of Younger Poets*, and *13 Pages*. Several of the poems in this collection were previously published in a pamphlet, *After the Creel Fleet* (Happen-stance, 2012). I would like to express my gratitude to the Society of Authors for the Eric Gregory Award I received in 2011, to the Robert Louis Stevenson Fellowship (2011) on whose residency some of these poems were written, and to the Arvon-Jerwood mentoring scheme (2013) for the help offered during this programme.

I would also like to thank the following people for their help, support and guidance: Patience Agbabi, Alison Angel, Neil Astley, John Glenday, Andrew Jamison, Roddy Lumsden and Helena Nelson. And thank you to my wife, Catriona McAra.

CONTENTS

Song

What sweeter triumph can there be
than the match lit in the grain-cellar,
no moon in the dark gallery
below the sleeping house. It's better

when I'm alone – can freely handle
those older tools for harrowing
and planting, turn the bent seed-cradle,
or thumb the axe-blade like a harp string.

Fleece

Given a choice of anyone unmentioned
in literary history, I'd sink
for a while into the stock frame of the shearsman
at Colchis – when they took the ram to him.

Such craft for the hands: leavening the gold
from the pale underskin; his head right down
to the knife line, he'd hear the whispered dub-
dub of the heart locked inside its red room.

The bats flown out above our tiny house,
I want to face the stiff wool folding back
on this his one, best hour: its golden sleeve;
the knife already blunting in his hand.

After the Creel Fleet

I never knew old rope could rust, could copper
in its retirement as a nest for rats.

The frayed lengths knotting into ampersands
tell of this night, and this night, and this,

spent taut between the surface and the sea-floor –
the water coarsening each coiled blue fibre

and strained, one strand might snap, unleash its store
of ripples to be squandered in the dark

though thousands would remain still intertwined
and thousands do remain, but frailer now.

These hoards, attached to nothing, not seen since
the last tightrope was walked, the last man hung.

On Eriskay

She met me at the fence. A kelpie
who'd stayed too long in this horse form,
she mouthed the sugar on my palm,
and when I slapped her barrel flank
the goose-moor stiffened with a sea
perfume. Gulls gathered on the stoop.

What a way to be seen out: confused
among the pearlwort and the fallow.
Her beach songs, like the recalled taste
of bucket milk, inched from her tongue.
Dusk grew behind the house. I watched
her drink the moon from a moon-filled trough.

The Tear in the Sack

A nocturnal bird, say a nightjar,
cocking its head in the silence
of a few deflowering trees,
witnesses more than we do
the parallels.
              Its twin perspective;
seeing with one eye the sack-
grain spilled on the roadway dirt,
and with the other, the scattered stars,
their chance positioning in the dark.

The Work

If I have to, then let me be *the whaler poet*,
launcher of the knife, portioning off
the pink cut, salt trim and fat, tipping
the larger waste off the side of the boat,
and then to have the poem in the drawer;

or, perhaps, let it be *the poet nurse*,
hearts measured by a small watch, balmer,
washer of old skin, stopping by the door
in the night –
                    or *the oil-driller poet*, primed
for the buried flame and heat, lips to the black,

aware how the oilfields in the evening
are lit like our own staggered desks.
Or, *the horse-trader* or *the smith*, or *the waiter poet* –
offering the choice wine, polishing to the light,
the bringer of the feast and the bill.

The Blackbird Singer

There we were at our hidden pastime:
one lugging a box and prop, another
who stole from a farmer's store the grain
that served as bait, and then the last
who'd imitate the call of a blackbird,
flirting them out from the bush.

The sound of beating wings. Such bliss
to listen to a sprung trap – our flawed
songbox that only played when shut,
so when you lifted the wood lip
from the pressed dirt its singer bolted
like a dark adolescent thought.

Back then, we heard of those who throttled
what they trapped – whose milk hands knew
the sureness of the yellow beak,
who would, then, skirt the stiffening frames
over the deep grass, the wings bent
on journeys always straight and short.

My brothers gone off for the night,
I'd stay to dream the symmetry
the act revealed: lifting the lid
to find the same song in the hands
as in the mouth – then the same silence
leaving the mouth as from the hands.

When the Whales Beached

On that day of spades,
engraving lines and inlets in the sand,

so that we could begin the slow
unmooring of those black shapes to the waves,

it was hard to think of anything
but how soon my grandmother

had followed her husband earthwards. Love,
and yet so much more than. The quiet

union of sometimes being the one
to lead, sometimes to follow. And these

who softly climbed the aching stair
of shore together, and didn't fall short.

How we stood by as if we'd nothing
to say, when, love, I did. I do.

Black Water

It's China that has, as the image of sleep,
the sleeper drinking from the night sea –
their bowl first lowered, and then raised with ocean;
a fisherman's son, I'm drawn to this.

Listening to the street's late deliveries,
I picture each one I love at this beach,
bowing intent to the work, their sand plot,
the moon adrift somewhere in their curved bay.

Here's my wife beside me, and there she is,
all lips and black water – I could ask,
where is my beach, my long sea? But, instead,
I'll raise this waking to my mouth, and drink.

The Winter Home

Darling, allow me the best evenings
to breathe the cold, to ruminate
like a diver on his rising breath.

The low-backed seat of the house step
inches ever further from the road.
And there's the jasmine opening

in garden branches. A white flower,
unfurling in the sub degrees,
in its pale rush of residing.

'The Letter Always Arrives at its Destination'

– then I wrote often to the sea,
to its sunk rope and its salt bed,
to the large weed mass lipping the bay.

The small glass bottles would be lined
along the bedroom floor – ship green
or church-glass clear – such envelopes

of sea-mail. Only on the day
of sending would a note be fed
into each swollen, brittle hull –

I had my phases: for so long
it was maps: maps of wader nests,
burrows and foxes dens, maps where

nothing was in its true position –
my landscape blooming from the surf.
Later, I'd write my crushes' names

onto the paper, as a small gift.
The caps then tested and wax sealed.
None ever reached my dreamed America,

its milk-white shore, as most would sink
between the pier and the breakwater,
and I would find that I had written

about the grass to the drowned sand,
again; and to the sunken dark,
I had sent all the light I knew.

Exchange Street

Blue ambulance lights beach against the streetlamps.
What a night to depart, with the first storm
of winter still a day from breaking and the town's
palest girl due to wear that reddest dress
she wears so seldom. Just imagine,
hung on to hear, perfected, from the window,
as the sleet falls, that hush in her red wake.

The Fraud

How like a shepherd or herdsman of loss
I must have whistled out into the evening
that a childhood dog came cowering to my heel:
years under, its coat now wool-thick with soil
and loosely collared with the roots of bog-myrtle.

A surprise then my old companion strained
to sneak by me to the fire and my wife.
Checked by a boot, it bore not a dog's teeth
but a long, black mouth. Then it slunk back to the hill.
Some nights I hear this thin dog claw the door.

Harvest

I've been thinking too much about the night
I slipped and the coal scattered on the snowed drive.

Then it was time spent in luck's appleyard
gathering its black fruit; or it was time

collecting what I'd left too long to gather,
a harvest all wilt and harrowed – anyway,

it was time spent, and I held the steel bucket,
filled it to the sound of nothing at all.

Return, Isle of Eriskay

Hardly a gesture at all but let me
twin the fact of the bay frozen over
with a light being in the window
of the abandoned house.

Let's talk of their comparable hush;
how, in its all year winter, plaster
snows from abandoned walls, and gathers;
how even when this cold the ice weeps.

Rodin Sculpts 'The Kiss'

There with a swung hammer is a man in love,
there's crafting, and there's breaking of squared marble.
There, the white dust and the scattered chippings
of what's fashioned out. How bare it looks,

half-made – a figure leaning in to kiss
what's not there yet, the arms encircling nothing
but a rougher offshoot of themselves. And yet
the kiss is held – as though the stone the figure

cradles receives it. Here is a strange knowledge
and a strange trust: his heart can sense the stone
heart aching in the block, his lips can taste
the mountainside that shapes into a mouth.

Grez, Near Dusk

Just a postcard to say not that it has rained
but that it smells impossibly of rain.

Moths feed on this silk hour, there's smoke from chimneys
where families are preparing for the change.

Let me explain how the bowed sky is heavy
with the deep-song of the failing colour

and yet it's missing. But stay. Wait with me.
Things will be different when the sun is lower.

Crossing

Say that the song was never written
would it have settled there, I wonder,
on that far shore of the tongue's river,
singing itself, stubbing its heels
into the bank that is pure air?

Or would it wait for further passage?
Stood on the quay so long until
a form all spit and bone and light.

Am I some whistling ferryman,
trailing my pen hand in the wake?

A Little Night Music

I've served apprentice to a watchmaker,
who knows how long – my job to pair
the wheel-cog to its pocketcase,

or, like a servant with a young prince,
to wash the little golden hands.
I dream of springs and time, and aiming

grit at a drum of brilliant darkness:
a game that starts the evening ticking.
Bowed over clockwork, the hour's stress,

I think about the night's stretched frame
and pockets full with the day's gravel:
so much is just this bearing stones.

Lyrebird

Owner of no plainsong,
it had come too late
to the song-box
on the first day

the other birds
having emptied it.
What a heart, then
or what a damn fool

to hear the axe-fall,
the back-firing car,
a world break apart
and think to sing it.

Concerning Song/Silence

Do you remember when he wrote
his weathered book of joy – and out

went the desk-lights above our own
thin books of shame, all wick and smoke,

and at no loss. For a moment it
was simple: an ink house, an ink

tree, blown to leaf, and the strange bird,
joy, shivering in the inked gorse.

Then, the head gathered some of what
the heart already knew of quiet:

the hush, the burr, the meadow-weed,
that this is all, and this enough.

For the Cold

The last tenant of our newest house,
had the gas boiler fire up in the late hours.
And so, last night, so cold, I listened to
the floorboards warp in the unwelcome heat.

I barely slept. The thought of him stretched out
beside us, hot as a hand that gives the slap.
Since then the water tenses in the pipe,
as his darkness changes to my dark.

Later Tasting

Who knows what he meant by that first-last gift
of grit and pollen and sheep-dirt, and rain,
and whatever was on the hand that picked them:
diesel, linen soap, fish blood, with peat crumbs
not emptied from the picking bucket.
The berries sieved beneath the garden pump.

Now pot, now jam-sugar and upper heat
and soon the felt cream lifted off, too sweet,
too sour, for tasting.
                    Bees strike against
the kitchen glass; nectar birds turn in the air
somewhere in their lost jungles. My grandfather,
knowing what a mouth is for, watches it cool

then asks to hold the bundle of his grandchild
and feeds this less-than-one year old, this milk child,
one teaspoon, and it shivers through the taste.

Today, I find another jar – still red
as a letter seal – and find it sweet, so sweet,
so sweet – and think I nearly understand him.

The Difficult

And since it's nearly always dark
here's thought, and not for those whose touch
or singing voice are as a brass lamp
gleaning the rock verge from the snow,

but for those pitch-and-wicker types,
who *take* so easily, whose warning
we steer by – even as it pours
from their mouths, pools in their cupped hands;

this burning that earns nothing but
the road ahead, the love of some.

Le Penseur

Perhaps I'm by the river, as the moths
for the seventh night in a week

emerge to butt the brightest windows,
the hot days gone by listening

to the rain-rhythms of the locals
and in practising my own line,

my *je ne comprends pas*,
assured as a bronze bell, and used

so often that they rightly wonder
what it is I do understand.

So, later, drafting a thinnest gospel
I'll versify the river and its passing,

the moths, their practice, and a bare sky.
Let them make of it what they will.

Sea Coins, Scottish Beach

Like rain's own tender fossil print;
or a drowned man's blue kiss, given over
to the great swell that took him home
by its straight and coldest route.

Oxidised copper: sweet, burdened trader;
purged of its minting date, its monarch,
everything but a bluest stamp,
that sets the borders of its country.

Advice on Love, Over Whisky

Northerner, I say never mind
that you've stood there with a sail
and not received one kiss of wind;
and your rain-water pail

has not been touched by rain;
distil, then, in a closed barrel:
be malt, be smoke, be the threshed grain
turned dark as caramel.

A Danse Macabre

(a mural for Eriskay Village Hall)

The tinker leads the way,
        tapping spoons, flourishing
his tin-hook tin-nail bracelets,
        burnt pots loll from his belt,

and the packman follows,
        hands flagged with penny hankies,
two-shilling cloths – a-grin
        with death – and pat-a-patting

the lost store of his suitcase,
        like a burst drum. Next peddlers,
boatmakers, farriers,
        swinging hands, fashioning

the night into a rough step,
        that leads to herring girls,
still gutting soft parts from
        slack fish, but loosening

their hips, as though they weren't
        now bed-promised to the sea.
Ahead the next loud troop
        comes the horse-charmer, flanked

by foals and mares – whose dance
        is stamped into the dirt.
And last the *seanchaidh*,
        stooped man, who shakes, turns, flails

like a wind-vane in the storm;
     dancing the same as all
of them: against the music,
     against the whole shamed dance.

packman: one who travels hawking cloths and linens;
seanchaidh: bardic storyteller.

Grez

There is the red-lit desk and wooden chair,
so now for evening's stove smoke, mothwork,
sun-in-the-leaves of the yard's birch. The quiet
that is Edith Piaf on a record player
a neighbour always lets turn at this hour –

and since that is my suitcase by the door
I'll drag it, as though it were an errant child,
to the stairwell, then the town limit, then
the short road of an empty railway platform.
There is the bending river by the hill
that I always saw – but, now, let me say
I saw it once, the hundred times the once.

A Porch-step Glossary for Smokers

Autumn: new-bag vanilla pipe tobacco
under the north city's long coat of rain.
My hours of connoisseurship have refined
to a series of beckonings and dismissals.

Leather and *liquorice*. The heavy flavours.
Then the sweet grained and green: *scratched lime, oak barrel,*
sent jostling with their hundred other songs
and their own dark cloud, past the homes of Knightswood.

When else (when awake) will one thing hold
so many hidden names? *Grass. Rust. The summer*
before the summer before the drought. And more
to be mined out, had I the hours or breath.

Epitaph

(for Calum)

The wind was carried on his voice
to Ruban and stone pier
and to the horses' fencing post;
the silence didn't care

for him, nor him for it. His church-bell
swung out for his long life;
only when night fell on the dark isle,
it tolled and cracked in half.

Forge

There you were, farrier and blacksmith,
who if called upon would have
gutted the house for metals, every
lock and moth-hinge.
                    The high tide of trade,
the toughening and night-work: shaping
your dark materials – horse-shoes, pins,
those small charms we fastened at the breast.

Walking Song

I didn't know there was a crossroads
until I stumbled onto it
or that this might have a slower road
till I mis-chose and travelled it;

I couldn't bear the forest's ditch-rose,
but wore the tired head of it,
I didn't know there was a right road
until I broke and strayed from it.

A Song for Rarity

(for E and A)

May you find pearlriver blooming
in your garden; and the evening-song fish
wrestling in your net; may thatch gulls
scatter like dice across the beach
at you and your partner's approach;
may your bed be made of blood oak,
and may you love well; may stonewater
fill your glass, and taste better than it should.

And This Was How It Started

The bet began when someone told the singer
he didn't know a thousand songs –
and his reply, cheered, was a ballad sung
about the foolish bet; the next praised wine,
and wine was poured and brought; and the third, sung
towards the barmaid, earned her troubled kiss.

Tally was chalked against the wall. Hours followed
of step songs, dancing tunes, until at dawn
he went through every rising hymnal – where
the sun was a balanced coin, god's thumbprint on
a tipping glass – though not a thousand songs
it was enough for us to claim him victor,

but on he went: day song, dusk song and night;
the boatmen's tunes, the Spanish elegies.
He stood, a hopeful groom, through his full day
of wedding hymns: the march, the kissing waltz
and bedding. After this he sang the spade
and earth of burials, fog on his breath.

Late on the fifth day, panicked by a silence,
he clicked and whistled through the blackbird's song,
the petrel's and the wren's – and we allowed it.
And then he sang the wave-fall when there's moonlight,
sang the black grain, its bending in the wind,
then sang the stars – and then, and then, and then.

An Introduction to the Gods of Scotland

Aberdeen

The eyeless. The enduring. The cautious that hid his great gifts, for the greater part, out of our reach. Who prefers his churches straight and grey. He is depicted always on the rock-face. He wears nothing but the grey doe-hide he skinned on the first day.

Edinburgh

In the beginning there was the stone, and this god of the rock quarry. It is tribute to him that candles and songbirds are lowered into mine shafts. Bridge builder. Castle founder. Do not look for him in the wood grain or the watermark. He reveals himself only in the grand. Moss has formed in his joints, his mouth, his eyes.

Glasgow

The god of the trafficker. She lent her tongue to the sea-bird, her strong arms to the haulier, her silver tongue to their custom-men. Who preached her own blasphemy – if only to hear her name on many tongues. Fickle. Strange. Mother to Babel and the high-rise. Never is the rain thought to be her remorse.

Dundee

The night god. His skin pale as shell. Built up his own high church only to misplace himself. The oldest. The frail and forgetful. Each of his twelve commandments trail off... By an error, he invented cannibalism. Often portrayed hunched over a star chart – trying to remember each constellation, why he had formed them, for whom.

Window, Honley

The village bell's been broken for a month,
sounding a flat, wrecked chime to the main hour;
the clapper between its iron walls sung out,

so I'll ask what time matters anyway:
just light, less light, and dark; the going off
of milk or love; our tides claimed back: weed rafts,

green wood and all; those old wolves disappearing
from the bleak forest that we dream about;
a town fire; a town flood; the marriage that

left confetti in the streets until the storm;
yesterday's sweet unrust; a man with pen
at a lit window, that he's long since left.

The House by the Sea, Eriskay

This is where the drowned climb to land.
For a single night when a boat goes down

soaked footprints line its cracked path
as inside they stand open mouthed at a fire,

drying out their lungs, that hang in their chests
like sacks of black wine. Some will have stripped

down to their washed skin, and wonder
whether they are now more moon than earth –

so pale. Some worry about the passage,
others still think about the deep. All share

a terrible thirst, wringing their hands
until the seawater floods across the floor.

The Songs of Kirilov

Rain in the air, the smoke rose and rose smoke;
the wife of the small town's perfumer dead,
how he burns her last clothes in the garden.
Their red hours he spent redressing the air
around her. Tonight, his evening breeze
although so painfully sweet, is still sweet.

*

My favourite thing: to go in the storm
to a town plantation, and watch the peach trees
suffer the gale coming for their soft globes.
Sat, soaked through, pocketing the rain,
knowing for the walk home there would be bruised fruit.
Unred, unripe. Just one will fill the palm.

*

The wolf stalked the winter forest,
its ribs a veiled fist. Tasted nothing
but the long empty plate of snow –
listening to the willow-weed,
the birch, the wind that runs through them.
Deciding just the same, that wolf
should be the last taste on a wolf's lips.

Reading Émile Zola, Grez

Somewhere out past the open window,
the mute's choir of thorn apple, honeysuckle,
and girls in red tops sleeping on thick grass,
face-down or face to the sun – teasingly
disclosing tender shapes they would take on
in a double bed, morning splayed across them.

Imagine me here, sat watching the village
like a village's illest child at my high window.
My bookish convalescence. A lone affront
to the sure and sun-kissed, the orange tree,
the blissful, heavy pollen of a hot day,
I measure my paleness against the clouds.

Carpenter's Studio off Exchange St

On the good evenings, I dream a ruined path
through dust and chipping; a hand raised to the plane
on the near wall. Strip timber will be thinned
at the long bench to something even light
could serve as prop to – task, please visit me;
this is the work, this is no work at all.

Leave Poetry

(after Luis Muñoz)

for those who are diminished or half-formed.
for those rare, unnamed birds on the bird-table.
for those who want to leave, but never do.
for those who talk, sing, curse, all without speaking.
for those who are alone.
for those who never share their evenings between two.
for those who, like mules, prefer the burden
and the journey through the unmapped provinces
of painful years, and don't search for their youth.

Leave poetry

for when you need the guide of its magnetic north.
for the nights you wake, your throat too dry
for prayer, it can be your water.
for times you need a second, imagined life,
or times you wish to sleep a restless sleep.
because it watches us even until death
with its unflickering eye, and open mouth
that sings of nothing but beauty.
for it gives us no explanations:
and this is sufficient:
and this is insufficient.
Leave poetry, my friend, for the shadows that retreat at morning.

Addendum

Do you recall how I told you of the woods
outside the French town: moth-heavy, a perfume

of sackcloth emanating from the scrub.
I add to this the dark bloom of a life

discovered, pursed and fat, beside the slope.
How I wish I'd cut it from the branch.

Smultronstället, Glendale

Will all this – ram's wool flagged on a neighbour's fence,
ash ruined grates, the wind-sprung thatch and gravel,
soon be recalled as wild strawberries were,
rain fattened, fast along his childhood's verge?
Something halts, hangs, stalls over those small hearts,
near lost, in long weeds; reaches out for them.

A Seal-skin Tale

My Version

This time there is no rockpooled shore,
no sealskin and no sealskin girl,
and never will the man make strides
across the sands that are not there.

This time, the story has not changed
despite there being no harr or thatch
or bracken – no strand, no wedding bed
for skin or shadows to lie on.

In fact, this time, there is no sun
to rise on anything, there's just
the sea and just the dark. I do
not know what story this is telling.

Kid

This is it, the true time, when little matters;
when the sun's dropped so low behind the hill
that the light fails, and doesn't mind its failing;

and art is just the kid by a now pink river
kicking stones out to mid-stream. Hey kid, dreamer,
here's a road and a tune, just whistle out

to dusk-fall – sometimes, the song carries; sometimes,
the shadow casts out longer than the man.

Juggler

I know the thing the apple passes through
between its peak and catch:

               and the small grace
collected in the collecting palm
and why the fruit must not be eaten later,

and I know the trembling and the risk,
the pardoning for stray light, winds, the audience,
and know the pact: that my hands finish
filled or empty – with neither feeling right.

North Atlantic Drift

We lay together in a run bath
and thought over the rowing boat
that neither one was rowing,

the evening berthed at the bath side
with its vowel song and habit
of staying with us for a while.

The low hall light behind us,
implied only where her breast,
her hip, undressed from the water.

That night the usual swell and drift
delivered my old spoilt thought
of whether a life like this is long

or long remembered – the shirts
receding in the corner shadows
dropped as weights, or anchorage.

Aesthetics, on a Side Street off Glasgow Green

The sky is starred by the shells of the Boches
The marvellous forest where I live is giving a ball
APOLLINAIRE, 'La Nuit d'avril 1915'

I will only be happy when I've withdrawn
at least a small way, to the Trongate
or to Watson Street, where the air, too,
stiffens with the influence of frost.

Glasgow shivers through its autumn mist
that knots with the fuse smoke of bonfire night.
Here the jacketed warm the underdressed,

shuffle between one spot beneath the dark
and another, waiting for the lights to begin;
while a girl somewhere is weeping in the crowd.

It's Apollinaire who's recalled saying, *war*
is a decidedly beautiful thing,
but then what's not, so far removed and holding
to the outskirts of everything: a bystander

to the blue noise of white vans passing by,
and those long shadows kissing at the wall.
Fireworks are sent into the air, fall over

the marvellous forest of the awed crowd,
and a girl with her head in her tiny hands.
The red sky doesn't mind if I say this.

Leave, Eriskay

I know the feeling of the grain farmer
who packed up and left his smallholding:
and not for the famine or the drought
but for the light being always on his back.